TALKING
SOCIAL JUSTICE

STORIES AND QUESTIONS FOR WORRIED,
WISTFUL, AND WOKE EVANGELICALS

HOWARD LAWLER

Salpizo Publications
Wake Forrest, NC

DEDICATION

To my son Jonathan who has always had my love but who has earned my respect as a man of God.

CONTENTS

Talk #16
Bowed heads and wistful eyes

Talk #17
Unpacking and washing

Talk #18
My father's fierce rebuke

Talk #19
Riotous confusion

Talk #20
It's a hashtag life

Talk #21
Receiving the face

Talk #22
The communism challenge

Talk #23
The wedding planners

Conclusion
Two endings

PREFACE
WHO IS TALKING?

"He who only says what others want to hear is better off remaining silent."

Ludwig Von Mises

I approached the police officer with a slow, deliberate tread. The decisive moment loomed. One question bore down on me: would the cop detect the two guns hidden under my jacket? I took one step closer.

Stop there. For now, I will say only two things about my experience described in those four sentences. First, that is exactly how things happened on a street corner in my inner-city neighborhood. Second, you must read beyond this preface to find out what happened. Leave that street corner for a bit while I tell you about this book.

It is storytime. None of the stories ahead are fiction. Some are from the Bible, some are from American history, and some are from my life. All lead to questions you can use to explore one of our culture's pressing issues: social justice.

We often hear politicians and pundits say that we "need to have a conversation about" some aspect of social justice. It seems to me that practically everybody is talking. I believe that we need *better* conversations. The church needs to have *deeper* conversations, rooted in the Bible. We cannot afford to skim the surface with slogans and simplistic notions.

Our approach to the Bible must be careful and reverent. We all make mistakes. Let us at least not make the mistake of being careless. We must take pains to handle the text accurately in context.

We dare not force God's word into our mold to make it do what we want. Even when our intentions seem noble that approach is insolent. In Zephaniah 3:1-5 the faithful prophet rebuked leaders who did "violence to instruction." That use of force is an injustice done to the living God who administers true justice. Those leaders did violence to God's word to cover their abuse of vulnerable people. We cannot take the same disreputable approach to God's revelation even when seeking to support vulnerable people.

My book's main value is presenting Bible passages that are often neglected or mishandled. The personal stories I tell and the history lessons I recite play a mere supporting role. The Bible is fully authoritative; the other stories are not.

The book's subtitle recognizes that evangelicals are worried about the issues in various ways. There is a lot at stake. Some are wistful for the good old days, perhaps of 1950s America. Some are woke and seek to apply Christian ethics as social justice warriors. All of us should examine God's perfect word – and then face the issues with grace and truth. The prophet Isaiah highlighted truth by writing, "Justice is turned back, and righteousness stands far off. For truth has stumbled in the public square, and honesty cannot enter. Truth is missing, and whoever turns from evil is plundered. The LORD saw that there was no justice, and he was offended" (Isa 59:14-15).

The stories in this book take about five minutes each to read. They are straightforward. The questions, however, are tricky and can lead to hours of talk. I designed them as discussion tools for you, not totems of my views on all matters. Please read the first appendix before you engage in any challenging conversations. You will find guidance from God's word there.

I focus on economics and race because they are the front-burner social justice topics. Other aspects of the topic come readily to mind, but I want to write a short book. I capitalize all racial labels

11

for consistency. It is the simplest approach and the most even-handed.

This book is a matter of personal stewardship. The Lord has provided experiences that help me foment conversation about social justice. Permit me to unpack my background a bit.

My parents grew up in true poverty. At best they flirted with the lower edge of the middle-class but got there by accruing significant credit card debt. I grew up living in flats and apartments.

Our neighborhood was rough at times. People tried to steal my bike twice while I was using it. In one instance, I stared down a guy holding a switchblade to my chest until he gave up. My parents told me I was wrong to take the risk – they could buy another bike but not another son.

I lived in a racially mixed community. My junior high graduating class was 40% Black, 32% Hispanic, 26% White, and 2% other ethnicities. Friends and foes ran the ethnic gamut. A Cuban girl sparked my first romantic feelings. I often spent time at the home of Puerto Rican friends eating and watching Spanish language TV (though I had little idea of what was said). My school lunch table crew was Black, Chinese, Hispanic, Indian, Irish (me), and Italian. I was menaced by Black, Hispanic, and White knife wielders.

I have been a pastor for almost four decades. You

can read some of my core doctrinal convictions in the second appendix. My goal is to serve the evangelical church which has traditionally embraced the positions stated in that appendix. The gospel forms our commonality.

I have enjoyed fellowship with people of all economic brackets and many races. A Jewish carpenter used a rough piece of wood and cold rock to build our bond. His work is worthy of full respect. I was made an honorary homeboy (their word, not mine) at a Black church, but it had nothing to do with race – I resonated with their Calvinistic leanings. Maybe I was destined for the honor. A Ladies Aid group proclaimed me an honorary Norwegian. Uff da!

History is my avocation. I read broadly, including works by Black authors such as Frederick Douglass, Booker T. Washington, Sojourner Truth, George E. Stephens, W. E. B. Du Bois, James Baldwin, Malcolm X, Julius Lester, Lucille Clifton, Wynton Marsalis, Thomas Sowell, and Barbara J. Fields. Such authors also include Augustine, Athanasius, and Tertullian.

My childhood experiences, my interest in history, and my pastoral ministry shape this book. I tell personal stories despite proper reticence to push myself forward. The social aspect of the topic makes personal testimony relevant. Indulge me that far, but focus on Jesus.

This book treads dangerous turf. Nerves are taught and frayed in our culture. I suspect the service I provide in these pages will discomfort people in all parts of my evangelical neighborhood. If you feel your hackles rising, please believe that I am trying to help.

This book is impressionistic rather than systematic or comprehensive. The diverse scenes flow back-and-forth chronologically and zoom in-and-out from personal history to world history. Do not look for a grand scheme. Just go with the flow. Ready?

TALK #1
DOWN ON THE CORNER

TRUE STORY

No dark or dangerous encounter went down on that corner. It was not the first time that I packed and approached that officer. It was all a game.

It was 1960, and I was four years old. Back then, kids playing with toy guns made no one reach for some antacid. I approached the policeman with two small cowboy pistols hidden in my jacket. His job was to spot them or frisk me to find them. As a well-trained officer, he always won the game. We both laughed. I was a happy loser.

The contest played out on the street corner of my home in Newark, NJ. The officer was a Black man. I am White. Skin hue did not matter to either of us. I never thought of him as being a different race. I could see our pigmentation mismatch, but that formed no barrier. All I recognized was my friend – "Fred the Cop." He granted me the liberty of calling him that despite his official status and my diminutive size.

For a slice of his day at work, Fred served as a traffic cop on our intersection. I played on the corner under my mother's supervision. On slower days he would tell my mom, "It's okay, Mrs. Lawler. Go inside. I will keep an eye on him." Not many kids have a babysitter bearing real firearms!

Eventually, we moved to another Newark neighborhood, and I lost contact with my impressive bodyguard. Fred had retired from the police and was working a part-time job as a salesman in a mall when my dad spotted him. We had a grand reunion. By then I knew how pigmentation divides people, as Fred had known. Our skin still formed no barrier.

I would have him watch my grandchildren in a heartbeat. I would love to meet him on a corner or in a store. I would say, "I am not packing any toy pistols today for you my friend – only affection and gratitude."

TALK AMONGST YOURSELVES

1. Does this story have any bearing on social justice?
2. Fred made more money and had more authority than my father. Did my dad enjoy White privilege compared to Fred?
3. What challenges do you think Fred faced as a police officer in a racially divided city?
4. Does the fact that I did not think of him as a Black person mean my parents trained me well?

TALK #2
BLACK, WHITE, AND BROWN

TRUE STORY

My father had one white arm and one brown arm. My mother often had black fingers. I will explain it all.

The three colors stem from one fact: neither of my parents went to high school. Lack of education, and other pressures, depressed their income prospects.

Start with mom. She was one of sixteen children (no typo there). All of them were single births and all delivered at home! The family lived in a small house on a dirt alley in Scranton, PA. The Great Depression often reduced the menu to potatoes and bread. Baths were in a tin tub with water heated from the stove. The kids shared a single stick of gum when they could get it, chewing it based on descending age. My mom, as one of the youngest, got her turn when all flavors had vanished. It was still a treat in her mind and mouth.

At sixteen, she moved to Newark, NJ, to live with her sister. She worked various jobs, sending almost all her earnings back to Scranton to help her family. She met and married a Newark native, and lived the rest of her life in the Garden State, but life was never a bed of roses.

Despite her childhood poverty, my mom ended up awash in jewelry. None of it was hers. She settled into a long stretch of polishing jewelry at a factory. Hence the black fingers. The polishing material worked its way deep into her fingers, leading her to soak them in bleach at times to remove the compound. She used special skin glue to close the resulting fissures.

Now for my dad. Pictures of him as a child appear to be from the set of The Little Rascals. He and his friends would roll downhill in old tires, and make various vehicles from boards, boxes, and baby carriage wheels. Though Irish, my father plucked chickens with the kosher butcher to pass time. He was delighted to get an orange at Christmas. His father had a decent job but spent a lot of his money buying drinks for friends at the local bar. (Feel free to make an Irish joke; I am not sensitive about my ethnicity). My grandmother hung curtains with string to make ends meet.

As for his white and brown arm tones, my dad spent most of his working life driving. Before vehicle air conditioning became common, he drove with the windows open all summer as he made deliveries.

The arm inside stayed white, while the one resting on the door turned red and then brown.

Mom and dad worked beyond retirement age and ended their days with no money to speak of, but they kept me and my sister well clothed and fed. They put a (rented) roof over our heads. They gave us fresh gum and much more than oranges for Christmas. They were far better providers and parents than either of them had known in childhood. As their offspring, our arms have always matched, and we never had to glue our fingers. Not bad after all.

TALK AMONGST YOURSELVES

1. Were you tempted to think any of the above was fiction? It is all true.
2. How would you plot my mom and dad on a scale for White privilege?
3. My parents never regarded their poverty as injustice. Should they have?

TALK #3
AD FONTES!

The insulated aluminum box stood sentinel on our front porch. I did not think much about it in my early years. I just knew that opening the lid in the morning meant getting milk. That was our routine in the city. Had I lived in the country I might have experienced milk's true source. That encounter was udderly beyond my frame of reference!

A famous Renaissance saying was, "Ad fontes!" – "Back to the sources!" It called for people to cease chewing the cud of second-hand notions, consume the original writings of philosophy, and ruminate on them. Sometimes going to the source makes a massive difference.

The prophet Habakkuk learned that lesson directly from God. Justice was the topic. The prophet's book begins with a complaining prayer in Habakkuk 1:2-4.

How long, LORD, must I call for help
and you do not listen
or cry out to you about violence
and you do not save?
Why do you force me to look at injustice?
Why do you tolerate wrongdoing?
Oppression and violence are right in front of me.
Strife is ongoing, and conflict escalates.
This is why the law is ineffective
and justice never emerges.
For the wicked restrict the righteous;
therefore, justice comes out perverted.

God answers the complaint in Habakkuk 1:5-11. He reveals the form of justice he planned, involving an utterly foreign and terrifying nation.

Look at the nations and observe –
be utterly astounded!
For I am doing something in your days
that you will not believe
when you hear about it.
Look! I am raising up the Chaldeans,
that bitter, impetuous nation
that marches across the earth's open spaces
to seize territories not its own.
They are fierce and terrifying;

their views of justice and sovereignty
stem from themselves.
Their horses are swifter than leopards
and more fierce than wolves of the night.
Their horsemen charge ahead;
their horsemen come from distant lands.
They fly like eagles, swooping to devour.
All of them come to do violence;
their faces are set in determination.
They gather prisoners like sand.
They mock kings,
and rulers are a joke to them.
They laugh at every fortress
and build siege ramps to capture it.
Then they sweep by like the wind
and pass through.
They are guilty; their strength is their god.

That response was not what the prophet expected. Continue reading his book to see him wrestle with God's approach.

God moves in mysterious ways. He would punish rampant injustice in the Promised Land by sending an enemy with self-sourced, warped ideas of justice! Eventually, it came to pass just as Habakkuk heard and recorded.

Eventually, I milked a cow. I met the source of

milk up close. It was an interesting experience. The cow probably found my rookie technique bothersome, but the encounter did not change either of our lives.

Another source changed my life and my eternity. Eventually, I accepted all that the Bible said about sin and salvation. I trusted Jesus for the gift of eternal life in my junior year of high school. I lapped up the milk of God's word about gospel basics (1Pet 2:1-3). I slowly but surely grew to digest the meat of the word about many matters (1Cor 3:1-4).

That is God's plan for every Christian. We do not automatically play our part. Hebrews 5:12-14 rebukes a lazy congregation, saying, "Although by this time you ought to be teachers, you need someone to teach you the basic principles of God's revelation again. You need milk, not solid food. Now everyone who lives on milk is inexperienced with the message about righteousness, because he is an infant. But solid food is for the mature – for those whose senses have been trained to distinguish between good and evil."

Do not chew the cud of contemporary culture about justice or anything else. Want to understand true justice? Be a Bible meat-eater. Go back to the source!

Talk amongst yourselves

1. How do you source your concept of justice?
2. How do you react to God's response to Habakkuk's complaint? Does it challenge your expectations?
3. Do people attribute god-like status to human ideas and abilities in contemporary calls for social justice?
4. How have you trained yourself to think biblically about justice and other matters?

TALK #4
MY MAJOR MISCALCULATION

TRUE STORY

People who know me now will struggle to believe the next sentence. When I was in junior high, I almost joined a gang.

As street gangs go, it was not much, but it was real enough to do damage. It was not race-based. The gang members were guys tired of being picked on. They were seeking a form of self-generated social justice.

"There is strength in numbers," I figured. I was bad at math, and my gang plan proved to be a massive miscalculation. I quickly dropped out of initiation for one main reason – the brick speech. The leader explained what he would do to me (or anyone else) who ran during a fight – "I will bash in your head with a brick." So I recalculated. I figured, "With friends like these...."

Suppose, however, that I could get one of the most powerful kings of history on my side. Then I would be set, right? No. A worship song from Israel tells us that is the wrong vector for the best help. The inspired song is Psalm 146.

> Hallelujah!
> My soul, praise the LORD.
> I will praise the LORD all my life;
> I will sing to my God as long as I live.
> Do not trust in nobles,
> in a son of man, who cannot save.
> When his breath leaves him,
> he returns to the ground;
> on that day his plans die.
> Happy is the one whose help is the God of Jacob,
> whose hope is in the LORD his God,
> the Maker of heaven and earth,
> the sea and everything in them.
> He remains faithful forever,
> executing justice for the exploited
> and giving food to the hungry.
> The LORD frees prisoners.
> The LORD opens the eyes of the blind.
> The LORD raises up those who are oppressed.
> The LORD loves the righteous.
> The LORD protects resident aliens
> and helps the fatherless and the widow,
> but he frustrates the ways of the wicked.

The LORD reigns forever;
Zion, your God reigns for all generations.
Hallelujah!

Kings and nobles fall short because they tumble into the grave and stay put. The psalm plots a higher plane for hope. King David knew his limits and said so in Psalm 145:14: "The LORD helps all who fall; he raises up all who are oppressed." David was obliged to pursue justice for all his people, and he did that well. But he never tried to be the hope of his people. He never tried to be God.

For any politician to assume a God-like stance is folly. To trust one in that role is double folly. You might as well take a brick to the head.

TALK AMONGST YOURSELVES

1. How much should we depend on political leaders to establish justice?
2. Have you heard anyone discuss this psalm when talking about social justice?
3. Does this psalm teach that citizens can be passive about exploitation, simply leaving victims to God's care?
4. How does our society violate the directive, "Do not trust in nobles, in a son of man, who cannot save"? How does the church do that?

TALK #5
FREE DISTRIBUTION

Let's take on another psalm. Psalm 112 links the rich and powerful with righteousness and justice. The whole psalm follows.

> Hallelujah!
> Happy is the person who fears the LORD,
> taking great delight in his commands.
> His descendants will be powerful in the land;
> the generation of the upright will be blessed.
> Wealth and riches are in his house,
> and his righteousness endures forever.
> Light shines in the darkness for the upright.
> He is gracious, compassionate, and righteous.
> Good will come to the one who lends generously
> and conducts his business fairly.
> He will never be shaken.
> The righteous one will be remembered forever.

He will not fear bad news;
his heart is confident, trusting in the LORD.
His heart is assured; he will not fear.
In the end he will look in triumph on his foes.
He distributes freely to the poor;
his righteousness endures forever.
His horn will be exalted in honor.
The wicked one will see it and be angry;
he will gnash his teeth in despair.
The desire of the wicked leads to ruin.

Even granting some poetic license to King David as a psalmist, his worship song makes claims that we cannot afford to write off as mere art. This psalm disallows simple identification of rich people with unrighteousness and of powerful people with injustice. I have never seen this psalm quoted in discussions on social justice. Maybe I missed it. Maybe not. People should at least give it attention, whatever they might make of it. Now that you have seen it, turn to the questions.

TALK AMONGST YOURSELVES

1. Do you temper or dismiss any of these positive statements about wealth and power as merely cultural? If so, how do you know biblical calls for just treatment of the poor are not simply cultural?
2. Does this passage guarantee riches to every faithful believer?
3. How do you relate this psalm's charitable free distribution to the idea of forced redistribution of wealth as an alleged act of justice?
4. Do you distinguish between wicked desires and wanting wealth?

TALK #6
BREATHTAKING RICHES AND JUSTICE

TRUE STORY

Hiking when out of shape, playing trumpet incorrectly, and getting punched in the gut have all taken away my breath. Gold never has. In the next account, a queen lost her breath, at least metaphorically. She gazed in wonder at gold that was no metaphor. She saw a lot more than that treasure. We will borrow her eyes to consider King Solomon's holdings and the issue of justice. In the interest of space, I now present the first nine verses of 1Kings 10, but I encourage you to read the whole chapter.

> The queen of Sheba heard about Solomon's fame connected with the name of the LORD and came to test him with difficult questions. She came to Jerusalem with a very large entourage, with camels bearing spices, gold in great abundance, and

precious stones. She came to Solomon and spoke to him about everything that was on her mind. So Solomon answered all her questions; nothing was too difficult for the king to explain to her. When the queen of Sheba observed all of Solomon's wisdom, the palace he had built, the food at his table, his servants' residence, his attendants' service and their attire, his cupbearers, and the burnt offerings he offered at the LORD'S temple, it took her breath away. She said to the king, "The report I heard in my own country about your words and about your wisdom is true. But I didn't believe the reports until I came and saw with my own eyes. Indeed, I was not even told half. Your wisdom and prosperity far exceed the report I heard. How happy are your men. How happy are these servants of yours, who always stand in your presence hearing your wisdom. Blessed be the LORD your God! He delighted in you and put you on the throne of Israel, because of the LORD'S eternal love for Israel. He has made you king to carry out justice and righteousness."

The chapter later says that Solomon perched on a grand ivory throne overlaid with fine gold. Household silverware did not exist because he went all gold for cups and such. The passage also tallies many other assets. He occupied the pinnacle of wealth and wisdom. Take it all in, take a deep breath, and then talk about it.

TALK AMONGST YOURSELVES

1. Why was Solomon praised for having great riches but judged by God for having many wives (See 1Kings 11)?
2. How do justice and massive wealth align in this passage?
3. Why is no correction given to the queen's perceptions?
4. How do you process 1Kings 10:23-24, which says, "King Solomon surpassed all the kings of the world in riches and in wisdom. The whole world wanted an audience with Solomon to hear the wisdom that God had put in his heart"?

TALK #7
CELEBRATING THE RICH

TRUE STORY

If this talk were a construction truck, you would hear beeping. We are in reverse. Back up two chapters in the Bible and visit a massive construction site.

King Solomon and his people dedicate a glorious new structure: the first Jerusalem Temple. God chose Solomon to build this magnificent worship center and Solomon did the job justice. We drop into the scene as Solomon begins a prayer of dedication in 1Kings 8:22-32.

> Then Solomon stood before the altar of the LORD in front of the entire congregation of Israel and spread out his hands toward heaven. He said: LORD God of Israel, there is no God like you in heaven above or on earth below, who keeps the gracious covenant with your servants who walk before you with all their heart. You have kept what you promised to

your servant, my father David. You spoke directly to him and you fulfilled your promise by your
power as it is today. Therefore, LORD God of Israel,
keep what you promised to your servant, my father
David: You will never fail to have a man to sit before
me on the throne of Israel, if only your sons take
care to walk before me as you have walked before
me. Now LORD God of Israel, please confirm what
you promised to your servant, my father David. But
will God indeed live on earth? Even heaven, the
highest heaven, cannot contain you, much less this
temple I have built. Listen to your servant's prayer
and his petition, LORD my God, so that you may
hear the cry and the prayer that your servant prays
before you today, so that your eyes may watch over
this temple night and day, toward the place where
you said, "My name will be there," and so that you
may hear the prayer that your servant prays toward this place. Hear the petition of your servant
and your people Israel, which they pray toward this
place. May you hear in your dwelling place in heav-
en. May you hear and forgive. When a man sins
against his neighbor and is forced to take an oath,
and he comes to take an oath before your altar in
this temple, may you hear in heaven and act. May
you judge your servants, condemning the wicked
man by bringing what he has done on his own head

and providing justice for the righteous by reward-
ing him according to his righteousness.

Skip to the conclusion of the celebration. Israel
was all in, as 1Kings 8:65-66 shows.

Solomon and all Israel with him—a great assembly,
from the entrance of Hamath to the Brook of Egypt—
observed the festival at that time in the presence
of the LORD our God, seven days, and seven more
days—fourteen days. On the fifteenth day he sent
the people away. So they blessed the king and went
to their homes rejoicing and with happy hearts for
all the goodness that the LORD had done for his
servant David and for his people Israel.

The living God of heaven was the star of the show
and the building took center stage on earth. Yet
Solomon was the people's choice for a rich round of
applause. They thanked God for the king and his success. People say that any friend can sympathize with
your failures, but a true friend sympathizes with your
success. Solomon had many true friends that day.

TALK AMONGST YOURSELVES

1. Should Solomon have gone to the Temple with the queen of Sheba so they could confess the sin of amassing wealth?
2. Should the poor in attendance have confessed the sin of celebrating the rich? Were they pawns duped by the ruling class?
3. How does the law against coveting your neighbors' possessions (Exod 20:17) relate to this issue?
4. What did justice mean in a social setting that was so economically stratified?

TALK #8
BAD TIMES AND
THE GOOD OLD DAYS

T$_{RUE}$ $_{STORY}$

Leap forward now about 200 years. Travel to the Promised Land during Isaiah's day.

The prophet gave Jerusalem worship services an epically bad review. He delivered one of the strongest rebukes God ever gave his people. Isaiah 1:10-23 delivers the bad news.

> Hear the word of the LORD, you rulers of Sodom! Listen to the instruction of our God, you people of Gomorrah! "What are all your sacrifices to me?" asks the LORD. "I have had enough of burnt offerings and rams and the fat of well-fed cattle; I have no desire for the blood of bulls, lambs, or male goats. When you come to appear before me, who requires this from you – this trampling of my courts? Stop bringing useless offerings. Your incense is detestable to me.

New Moons and Sabbaths, and the calling of solemn assemblies – I cannot stand iniquity with a festival. I hate your New Moons and prescribed festivals. They have become a burden to me; I am tired of putting up with them. When you spread out your hands in prayer, I will refuse to look at you; even if you offer countless prayers, I will not listen. Your hands are covered with blood. Wash yourselves. Cleanse yourselves. Remove your evil deeds from my sight. Stop doing evil. Learn to do what is good. Pursue justice. Correct the oppressor. Defend the rights of the fatherless. Plead the widow's cause. "Come, let's settle this," says the LORD. "Though your sins are scarlet, they will be as white as snow; though they are crimson red, they will be like wool. If you are willing and obedient, you will eat the good things of the land. But if you refuse and rebel, you will be devoured by the sword." For the mouth of the LORD has spoken. The faithful town – what an adulteress she has become! She was once full of justice. Righteousness once dwelt in her, but now, murderers! Your silver has become dross to be discarded, your beer is diluted with water. Your rulers are rebels, friends of thieves. They all love graft and chase after bribes. They do not defend the rights of the fatherless, and the widow's case never comes before them.

I have heard evangelicals cite this passage to call the church to fight the economic stratification of American society. Some use this text to advance a form of democratic socialism. We must all pay close attention to what pursuing justice means in the context.

The passage says Jerusalem was once full of justice and was the home of righteousness. That reference to the good old days looks back to David's reign. But the king lived in an opulent palace while others lived in poverty. Impoverished Israelites gleaned grain from the edges of fields as the Law directed (Lev 23:22). It seems that economic leveling was not on the agenda for God's nation.

People praised David and his reign. Israel's worship songs (the Psalms) celebrated him as a righteous king, blessed by God. Some people say that we see what God thinks about money when we look at the people to whom he gives it. In David's case, he gave a lot of it to a noble soul.

Look again at the beginning of the above Bible passage. We, too, must hear the word of the Lord as we deal with money and much more.

TALK AMONGST YOURSELVES

1. How should the context shape evangelical use of this passage in social justice discussions?
2. David was one of the richest people in history. Did that make him an oppressor of the poor in his kingdom? If so, why does the prophet Ezekiel make a stark distinction between David and the "fat" and "strong" leaders who abused Israel (Ezek 34)? Why does the Apostle Paul (in Acts 13) describe David as a man after God's own heart who had served his generation according to God's will?
3. Isaiah's language comes from the courts of Israel. How does the focus on equal treatment in the courtroom relate to the broad cultural engineering now associated with social justice?
4. Suppose the church somehow cleansed all American courts of partiality and abuse. Would that satisfy the concerns of Isaiah 1? What if the gap between the poor and the wealthy citizens remained?

TALK #9
THE INNOCENT POOR

TRUE STORY

The people paid little heed to Isaiah. Idolatry formed one of their worst sins. In Isaiah 40, the prophet condemns various idolaters. In verse 20 he notes, "A poor person contributes wood for a pedestal that will not rot. He looks for a skilled craftsman to set up an idol that will not fall over." The impoverished person had no gold or marble but still made an idol with materials at hand.

The idolatry plague persisted into the next century when the prophet Jeremiah served God. In Jeremiah 2:31-35, we find another stinging rebuke.

> Evil generation, pay attention to the word of the LORD! Have I been a wilderness to Israel or a land of dense darkness? Why do my people claim, "We will go where we want; we will no longer come to you"? Can a young woman forget her jewelry or a

bride her wedding sash? Yet my people have forgotten me for countless days. How skillfully you pursue love; you also teach evil women your ways. Moreover, your skirts are stained with the blood of the innocent poor. You did not catch them breaking and entering. But in spite of all these things you claim, "I am innocent. His anger is sure to turn away from me." But I will certainly judge you because you have said, "I have not sinned."

The phrase, "the innocent poor" implies the opposite – the guilty poor. This aligns with Isaiah who talked about ungodly orphans and widows (Isa 9:17). The law forbade favoring the poor as well as the powerful. Leviticus 19:15 says, "Do not act unjustly when deciding a case. Do not be partial to the poor or give preference to the rich; judge your neighbor fairly."

Jeremiah invited people to explore poverty and justice in Jerusalem. In Jeremiah 5:1-6, he does not exempt the poor from God's indictment.

Roam through the streets of Jerusalem. Investigate; search in her squares. If you find one person, any who acts justly, who pursues faithfulness, then I will forgive her. When they say, "As the LORD lives," they are swearing falsely. LORD, don't your eyes look for faithfulness? You have struck them, but they felt no pain. You finished them off, but they refused to accept discipline. They made their faces harder than rock, and they refused to return. Then I thought: "They are just the poor; they have been foolish. For they don't understand the way of the LORD, the justice of their God. I will go to the powerful and speak to them. Surely they know the way of the LORD, the justice of their God." However, these also had broken the yoke and torn off the chains. Therefore, a lion from the forest will strike them down. A wolf from arid plains will ravage them. A leopard stalks their cities. Anyone who leaves them will be torn to pieces because their rebellious acts are many, their unfaithful deeds numerous.

Jeremiah's initial orientation was to temper his disappointment with the poor and to expect better things of the powerful. In the end, he did not hold a sentimental (or cynical) view of the poor or the powerful. The poor who broke God's yoke and the powerful who did so all bore responsibility. Conduct mattered, not category (see Ezek 18). That is justice.

I have not heard Christians address the above passages when conversing about social justice. Ponder these texts and proceed to the questions.

TALK AMONGST YOURSELVES

1. Have you covered these passages in conversations about the issues?
2. Do you assign virtue to people simply because they are poor? Or, in the opposite direction, do you assign guilt to people just because they are poor?
3. If poor people are caught breaking and entering, should they pay a penalty, or are they automatically justified because of poverty?
4. What idolatries might poor people find tempting today?

TALK #10
JOSIAH, JEHOIAKIM, AND JUSTICE

TRUE STORY

Jeremiah never stared down a guy with a switch-blade. The prophet did something more deadly – he told the hard truth to a king. That could cut short one's ministry, but God protected Jeremiah through many confrontations.

In one sanctified rumble between the prophet and a potentate, Jeremiah upbraided King Jehoiakim. He reprimanded the royal about his palace and poor performance of justice. We read all about it Jeremiah 22:13-23.

> Woe for the one who builds his palace through un-righteousness, his upstairs rooms through injustice, who makes his neighbor serve without pay and will not give him his wages, who says, "I will build myself a massive palace, with spacious upstairs rooms." He will cut windows in it, and it will be paneled with

cedar and painted bright red. Are you a king because you excel in cedar? Didn't your father eat and drink and administer justice and righteousness? Then it went well with him. He took up the case of the poor and needy; then it went well. Is this not what it means to know me? This is the LORD'S declaration. But you have eyes and a heart for nothing except your own dishonest profit, shedding innocent blood and committing extortion and oppression. Therefore, this is what the LORD says concerning Jehoiakim son of Josiah, king of Judah: They will not mourn for him, saying, "Woe, my brother!" or "Woe, my sister!" They will not mourn for him, saying, "Woe, lord! Woe, his majesty!" He will be buried like a donkey, dragged off and thrown outside Jerusalem's gates. Go up to Lebanon and cry out; raise your voice in Bashan; cry out from Abarim, for all your lovers have been crushed. I spoke to you when you were secure. You said, "I will not listen." This has been your way since youth; indeed, you have never listened to me. The wind will take charge of all your shepherds, and your lovers will go into captivity. Then you will be ashamed and humiliated because of all your evil. You residents of Lebanon, nestled among the cedars, how you will groan when pains come on you, agony like a woman in labor.

Telling a king he merited a donkey's funeral is a risky business. Jehoiakim's eyes worked well enough to read the prophet claim the king had a hearing problem. Let's do better.

Talk amongst yourselves

1. Can one build a palace through righteousness? Did anyone do that in the Bible?
2. What distinguished the palace-dwelling father from the cedar-loving son? For background, read 2Kings 22.
3. The text says that knowing God means doing justice. Does doing justice always mean knowing God?

TALK #11
ALIENS AND A JUST SOCIETY

TRUE STORY

Now consider all the Bible passages that call the Israelites to establish justice in society while in exile. There – we are done. Every time a prophet commanded the Jewish people to establish (or re-establish) systematic justice in society, the people lived in the land of their inheritance.

Daniel and Ezekiel are the two exilic prophets. Daniel does not address social justice. When exiled Ezekiel writes about justice, he only comments on what had happened, or was happening, in the Promised Land. He did not give his fellow Jews the mission to make Babylonian society just.

The prophets said the Jewish people must produce justice when they were residents in their land. Isaiah 1, for example, mentions their nation and their land as it rebukes Israelite injustice in verses 1, 3, 4, 7, 8, 19, 21, 24, 26, and 27. Evangelicals often neglect this context when linking prophetic calls for justice to contemporary societies.

Some say that the church's mission mirrors the Israelite responsibility for justice, but neglect noting the change the Jewish people experienced during exile. Abuse of aliens in the Promised Land was a prime factor for the punishment they received. But God does not task them with social reform when they were aliens. The covenant land and the land of exile are not the same things (2Chron 6:38-39). Their land was a theocracy in which they could set the terms for society under God. The land of exile was far from their land in every way.

The New Testament calls the church aliens and exiles on the earth. Hebrews 13:14 tells the church, "For we do not have an enduring city here; instead, we seek the one to come." Consider also 1Peter 2:9-12.

> But you are a chosen race, a royal priesthood, a holy nation, a people for his possession, so that you may proclaim the praises of the one who called you out of darkness into his marvelous light. Once you were not a people, but now you are God's people; you had not received mercy, but now you have received mercy. Dear friends, I urge you as strangers and exiles to abstain from sinful desires that wage war against the soul. Conduct yourselves honorably

among the Gentiles, so that when they slander you as evildoers, they will observe your good works and will glorify God on the day he visits.

Our land is not here. No geographic spot on this globe qualifies. 1Peter 1:4-5 says God has given Christians a living hope, "into an inheritance that can never perish, spoil or fade—kept in heaven for you, who through faith are shielded by God's power until the coming of the salvation that is ready to be revealed in the last time." Our covenant land is the new heavens and the new earth. Until then, we pass through every land.

Exiles should not be indifferent about the good of society. The Jewish exiles were told to pray for the land of their exile and to seek its well-being (Jer 29:4-11). Strangers and aliens do not withdraw in the church age either. We must pray for leaders (1Tim 2:1-2). Paul used Roman citizenship as a good steward and we must use our civic privileges well. Do that, but never try to build a home on land not your own.

TALK AMONGST YOURSELVES

1. How do Christian aliens properly pursue justice?
2. What is our responsibility in a democratic republic? What responsibility does a local church bear?
3. What does being a "chosen race" mean, and how does it shape our view of current racial issues?
4. Do you picture God (apart from the Lord's incarnation as a Jewish man) in racial imagery?

TALK #12
COMING TO TERMS WITH TERMS

TRUE STORY

Next, we will look at all the times the Bible uses the term "social justice." That was quick work. We are finished.

We do not find the term "social justice" in the Scriptures. That does not make it an anti-biblical term. Many useful words are not in the Bible: fondue, piano, Buick, dentist, pizza, and polymer. Sound theological terms not in the Bible summarize teaching that is: hypostatic union, imprecatory psalm, inerrancy, omnipresence, theocracy, and Trinity.

All justice is social in theory and practice, so the adjective seems nonessential. "Social justice" first appeared (as far as I can tell) in the mid-1800s. Social theories shifted away from personal virtue to structures. The goal of revamped structures became equal outcomes, not equality under the law, as in the Bible. "Social justice" today can indicate the government-driven pursuit of utopian goals. That pursuit and the practice of equal treatment under well-conceived laws significantly diverge.

The cultural social justice agenda now in play often opposes God's will revealed in scripture, fairly interpreted in context. Some activists undermine monogamous, heterosexual marriage and the nuclear family. Some support abortion. Killing 60 million vulnerable human beings since Roe v. Wade is at odds with biblical anthropology.

People dip into passages like Amos 2:7 for a "social justice" quote. The prophet judges Judah, saying, "They trample the heads of the poor on the dust of the ground and obstruct the path of the needy." Quote in hand, they dismiss the inconvenient statements in the remainder of the verse. The prophet immediately links sexual morality with justice, saying, "A man and his father have sexual relations with the same girl, profaning my holy name."

The book of Isaiah talks about salvation through justice. Like other prophets, Isaiah platforms God's wrath against sin as a prime expression of justice. Even salvation emerges from God's justice. The people filling social media do not seem to note that facet of justice when they quote Isaiah or other prophets.

When Calvin and other reformers talked about a well-ordered society, they did not talk about social justice. They spoke about "civil righteousness" and "virtue." They based those concepts on the Ten Commandments. Progressive social and political platforms are differently sourced.

One day a friend said to me, "There is no such thing as social justice, there is only justice and injustice." His simple words made me think. I have not stopped. Think a bit yourself, and tackle the following questions in conversation.

TALK AMONGST YOURSELVES

1. Do you think the adjective in "social justice" is helpful?

2. Does the current pursuit of social justice favor some groups over others? Can you think of groups that suffer injustice because of social justice?

3. If you use the term "systemic racism" do you have a clear meaning in mind? What evidence is required to charge a culture with being systemically racist? What could an individual or a church do about it?

4. If people used the term "social engineering" instead of "social justice," what would result?

TALK #13
A PRO-SLAVERY BIBLE?

TRUE STORY

No institution blights American history like slavery. Military conquest, debt, and criminal penalty drove slavery in the ancient world. Rank prejudice fueled the American form. Alexander Stephens, the Vice President of the Confederacy, made the racial basis clear in his "Cornerstone Speech" on March 21, 1861, in Savannah, Georgia. He said that the Confederate Government was founded on the moral truth that Black people were not equal to White people. He claimed slavery is the natural condition for Blacks.

Some back then sought to buttress that position by using the Bible. But slavery is not a creation ordinance. God started with Adam & Eve – not Adam & Eve & Spartacus. Slavery emerged in a fallen world and expresses disorder. The book of Revelation does not show slavery as part of the new heavens and earth to come.

There is no positive doctrine of slavery in the Bible. The law carefully regulated it due to the inherent danger of abuse. Six years was the slavery service limit for Israelites, though an Israelite could choose to remain a slave (Deut 15:12-18). Only non-Israelites could be slaves for life (Lev 25:39-46). The Apostle Paul advised slaves to become free if possible (1Cor 7:21).

It is impossible to justify the racial component in our history by contextual use of the Bible. Many Christians (North and South) trumpeted that fact at the time. Those who claimed the Bible supported the American form of slavery did not follow all that the Bible says. The Fugitive Slave Act of 1850 forced Northerners to return escaped slaves. But Bible-quoting slaveholders did not mention Deuteronomy 23:15-16, which says, "Do not return a slave to his master when he has escaped from his master to you. Let him live among you wherever he wants within your city gates. Do not mistreat him."

In the early church, slaves and masters (such as Onesimus and Philemon) were members of the same local assembly. American slavery kept Blacks out of White churches. That state was true in many Northern churches as well. Or, as ill.

Paul brought Christian humility to bear on slavery in the case of individual believers and local churches.

The spread of the gospel weakened slavery in the Roman world and beyond. Christianity drove the demise of slavery in Western culture. At no time in history did the church universally teach that slavery was a good thing. It is always a good thing, however, to apply the eternal gospel to our relationships.

TALK AMONGST YOURSELVES

1. It is easy to disdain slaveholders. But do you harbor any of the prejudice that drove American slavery?
2. Can you think of other cases where Bible texts became pretexts to support unworthy positions? Can you think of any involving modern social justice?
3. Are we justified in misusing the Bible for a perceived good result?

TALK #14
GO FIGURE

TRUE STORY

He could fall asleep in minutes, on plain dirt, and during chaos. He was on the ground again, and he appeared dead to the world during more chaos. That was appropriate in one way – he had been dead for 135 years. His name is Ulysses S. Grant, and his statue just hit the dirt in a California park as an act of alleged social justice.

I suppose it makes sense. After all, he did marry a slaveholder. He even owned a slave at one time.

No, it does not make sense. If you pay attention to the whole story, you see the protestors were miserably short-sighted.

Yes, Grant married a slaveholder. He fell in love in a day where deeply flawed ideas about race were common. His wife, Julia, suffered skewed vision due to a misaligned eye. A lot of people had a skewed view of race then, and slavery was one nasty result. His union with Julia caused friction with Grant's abolitionist family. His wife's family never accepted him as one of their own.

Yes, Grant had owned one slave. His father-in-law gave the slave to him to work a patch of land when Grant had no money and no prospects. Grant offended his White neighbors by working side-by-side with the slave. The market said the slave was worth about $30,000 in today's currency. Grant did not sell the man or rent him to others. He set William Jones free on March 29, 1859.

What else did the protestors miss due to their rage-induced myopia? Grant became an avowed abolitionist. Grant did the most of any general to destroy the institution of slavery by military means. As President, Grant sent the military to fight the Ku Klux Klan and almost destroyed it. Grant signed the 15th Amendment into law which gave Blacks the right to vote. He called the law the most important event in the nation's history. Grant appointed many Blacks to important government positions. For all his trouble righting wrongs, he received numerous death threats.

Go figure. That is what the protestors were saying as they looked on the figure of U. S. Grant in that park. To them, the statue had to go. They need to go figure out who they just toppled. They do not need to put the man on a pedestal. They should, however, put him in perspective. So should we.

TALK AMONGST YOURSELVES

1. Can anyone (besides Jesus) look back on a life with no flaws?
2. Israel celebrated King David even though he murdered Uriah to gain the good soldier's wife for himself (2Sam 11-12). Should Israel have disowned David?
3. Does Ulysses Grant merit a statue in light of his service and virtues?
4. Who gets to pick which statues stand and which fall? Would the park protestors like to pose for a statue?

TALK #15
SOME GRAVE QUESTIONS

TRUE STORY

I sit four feet away from a tombstone as I type this sentence. It hangs on the wall in my office. Gravity is not an issue. To be precise, I sit near a rubbing made from a headstone. The name rendered in relief represents my relative. The man in that grave raises some weighty questions.

Stillman R. Doty was born in 1830 and served in the 28th New Jersey Volunteer Infantry Regiment during the American Civil War. He survived the war and died in 1898. My father's family chose Corporal Doty's first name to serve as my dad's middle name. My cousin made the monument rubbing for us when she located the veteran's grave.

Despite the family connection, we do not know much about that Union volunteer. The big question looms unanswered: why did he fight? Did he endure the deprivations and horrors of war because he wanted to help free slaves, as many White and Black soldiers did? Did he unintentionally help free the slaves despite being a racist, as many White racists north of the Mason-Dixon line did? We do not know if either of those stories (or some other) is true.

We only know that our relative wore the blue uniform and helped put an end to a heinous institution. For that much, I am grateful. Beyond that, more questions loom. Try a few of them on for size now.

Talk amongst yourselves

1. Hundreds of thousands of people died in a war that ended slavery as an institution. What role does that play in current relations between Black and White people?
2. If Stillman Doty fought because he was an abolitionist, do justice credits (akin to carbon offsets) accrue to me?
3. If he fought despite being a racist, what should I think and feel about my connection to him and race relations today?
4. Ezekiel 18 assigns guilt to individuals, not to generations. What bearing does that approach have on the issue of American slavery?

TALK #16
BOWED HEADS AND WISTFUL EYES

Since the late 1700s, Christians have sung about casting wistful eyes (the lyric is also rendered "wishful eyes") toward our Promised Land in heaven. "Wistful" means nostalgic, which involves gazing back. The gospel creates a longing for a beloved home we have not yet visited.

Evangelical Americans sometimes cast wistful eyes in the usual direction, back to some preferred time when things were better, perhaps the 1950s. We might long for the return of prayer and Bible reading in public schools, organized by those schools. The Supreme Court ended that practice in 1962. No longer do public school teachers direct children to bow their heads in class. Silent prayer during tests still happens.

I do not deny that some things were better in the 1950s, but I am not wistful about the era. I made my appearance midway through the decade, so I have few memories of that time to fuel nostalgia. But there is more to my stance as I glance back.

I have seen photos of bowed heads that pain me – people in 1950s America bowed over public drinking fountains. The sign over one fountain says "White"; the sign over the one next to it says "Colored." The White fountain is often modern and attractive, unlike the other, adding insult to injury. If you want to plunge into one painful episode from the not so happy days, read about Bloody Tuesday on June 9, 1964.

I find it hard to fathom that segregating sipping was alive and unwell during my brief lifetime. What a disgrace! The Civil Rights Acts of 1964 outlawed the practice. A Democrat president signed the law after a Democrat senator (and former Klansman) spoke against the bill for over 14 hours. No political party had a monopoly on virtue.

Suppose I had the power to bring back state-sponsored prayer in public schools. I could cast a spell that made it happen with one proviso: segregated water fountains would also return. No way.

I cast my wistful eye forward to the Promised Land. People of every kind "will no longer hunger; they will no longer thirst; the sun will no longer strike them, nor will any scorching heat. For the Lamb who is at the center of the throne will shepherd them; he will guide them to springs of the waters of life, and God will wipe away every tear from their eyes" (Rev 7:16-17). That is no wish. That is a promise.

TALK AMONGST YOURSELVES

1. Ecclesiastes 7:10 tells us, "Don't say, 'Why were the former days better than these?' since it is not wise of you to ask this." How does that relate to the above story?
2. Black visitors could not stay in any of Gettysburg's 30-plus hotels and boardinghouses in the mid-1900s. Do you detect the irony?
3. Are you ever selectively wistful?
4. How does the prospect of a vast multitude from every nation, tribe, people, and language worshiping the Lamb together shape your conduct now?

TALK #17
UNPACKING AND WASHING

TRUE STORY

My friend was a fine pastor. He was a quiet and gentle person, but unafraid of touching sore spots in the line of duty. One Sunday he did that with remarkable results.

He led a largely White congregation. The small church was in a community that had shifted demographics over the decades from White to mostly Black and Hispanic. The congregation did not look like the neighborhood anymore. My friend cared about the community and did not want race to impede the gospel ministry.

So, he touched a sore spot. He made no assumptions about anyone based on race but raised the issue of racial prejudice. It is always a relevant concern. I doubt any of us has met anyone who never harbored an uncharitable thought about one group or another.

The pastor asked his flock to examine their hearts

before the Lord. One long-term member talked to him after the service and assured the pastor that he was not prejudiced. He offered stone-cold proof. He told my friend that he had just been to the supermarket that week and that a Black person had packed the bags at the check-out lane. Then came the proof. Brace yourself. He told my friend that he unpacked the bags at home and did not even wash his hands! I do not write fiction. Even if I did, I doubt I could have created that outrageous line.

End this true story by reading some pure lines from God's word.

Psalm 139:23-24: Search me, God, and know my heart; test me and know my concerns.
See if there is any offensive way in me;
lead me in the everlasting way.

Mark 7:4, 20-23: When they come from the marketplace, they do not eat unless they have washed. And there are many other customs they have received and keep, like the washing of cups, pitchers, kettles, and dining couches...And he said, "What comes out of a person is what defiles him. For from within, out of people's hearts, come evil thoughts, sexual immoralities, thefts, murders, adulteries, greed, evil actions, deceit, self-indulgence, envy, slander, pride, and foolishness. All these evil things come from within and defile a person."

Ask God to unpack our hearts about prejudice whatever our races may be. His truth and grace are the best cleaners in the world.

TALK AMONGST YOURSELVES

1. What would you have done if you were in that pastor's place? Would you preach as he did? What would you have said to that congregant?
2. Do you harbor any prejudice in your heart toward any group?
3. Does our culture tend to approve of prejudice toward some groups yet not of others? Is that justice?

TALK #18
MY FATHER'S FIERCE REBUKE

TRUE STORY

"Easy going" – that label describes my dad. Yet, he had a firm sense of right and wrong. When he saw injustice, he became decisive, proactive, and resolute. One day, I was on the receiving end of that part of his persona. He fired a shot across my bow with a rebuke designed to change my course. It worked.

I had done something that was out of character. I made an insulting comment about Black people. Dad instantly told me that comment was unacceptable. I should have known better. He was known to go toe-to-toe in battle when my grandfather made racist comments.

Before you judge my dishonorable speech that day, listen to the back story. I had a two-block walk home from junior high school. One day it proved a block too far. I exited the school from the rear after band practice and went up an alley to the street. Eight Black kids immediately started chasing me. I got halfway home when they got me. They beat me up. As we tussled, I knocked the hat off one and stomped it in a puddle. That made matters worse. One guy busted a thick stick on my head. Then another spotted my trumpet case, opened it, and they all ran off with the prize.

I made my racist comment to my dad right after that. My words emerged in the flush of fear, pain, and anger. Even in that context, my father issued his fierce rebuke about racist language.

The main assailant was identified. Weeks after the robbery, he told a court why the group pounced. He said, "We were sitting around, and someone said, 'Let's beat up the next White boy that comes along.'" I was the unlucky winner of that lottery.

My father heard that testimony in the courtroom. It produced no change in my dad's behavior. He did not condemn a race for the crime committed against me or excuse the crime by citing race.

In our family court, I remained under the ban forbidding the type of comment I ventured right after the attack. My dad's manner told me he was not fooling. I heeded the warning. I returned to my characteristic speech, which does not denigrate groups or individuals based on race.

I would rather not have entered the school alley or the footrace on that fateful day. I wish I did not utter my derogatory remark. But I am delighted that God, in his providence, gave me a kind, firm father with an abiding sense of justice.

TALK AMONGST YOURSELVES

1. Are there any racists in the above account?
2. Do I still bear guilt for my comment or did my repentance clear accounts on that score?
3. What role should justice play in cases of assault and robbery between people of different races?

TALK #19
RIOTOUS CONFUSION

TRUE STORY

The enraged White mob lynched many Black people in the four-day calamity. A partially disabled coachman named Abraham Franklin was easy prey. The mob hung the man from a tree as they cheered for Jefferson Davis, president of the Southern Confederacy. Thugs cut down Franklin's dead body and dragged it through the streets.

The city was not south of the Mason Dixon line. Manhattan hosted the mayhem. The race-based murders happened in the draft riots of July 13-16, 1863. Good order was not fully restored until five Union regiments arrived in New York City from the battle of Gettysburg.

My distant Irish kin committed most of the murders. Many Irish suffered from deep poverty. Some White people hated them, considering them another race. Some Anglo Americans threatened the Celtic immigrants to suppress their votes. Many Whites deemed the Irish to be worthless. Slaveholding Whites would hire Irish workers to spare slaves from the most dangerous jobs. One Alabama riverboat owner explained why, saying that when the Paddies broke their backs or fell overboard, nobody lost anything. The Irish displayed similar prejudice at times. In the 1900s, some Irish immigrants in New York City regarded Italians as non-White and worthless.

The Irish proved valuable to the Union war effort. Irish regiments won more decorations and suffered more losses than others. Yet, many Irish were furious in Manhattan by 1863. They resented being drafted to fight for emancipation. Anger erupted in murder, and many Black people fell as victims.

Standing against the angry Irish mob were... Irish people. Many of the police were Irish. One-hundred-and-fifty members of the Eleventh New York Volunteer Infantry helped the police to fight the mob. The unit commander was an Irishman named H. J. O'Brien. After dispersing one pack of rioters, Colonel O'Brien went to his home in Manhattan to check on his family. A crowd savagely beat him, dragged him through the streets, dropped him in his front yard, stabbed him, and stoned him. It took several hours for O'Brien to die.

Confusion of all sorts surrounded slavery and race relations. In the 1830s in South Carolina, hundreds of free Black people owned Black slaves, many Whites owned no slaves, and other Whites opposed slavery. Indians practiced slavery on each other long before Europeans came to this land. Some tribes enslaved Blacks. Indians fought for both the Confederacy and the Union during the Civil War.

There is an Irish joke about confusion. One Irishmen spotted a mirror on the road, picked it up, and said, "That man looks familiar." The other one grabbed the mirror, looked in it, and said, "Of course he does. That's me!"

Some confusion is riotously funny. The draft riots were brutally ugly. They form a cultural mirror that holds some valuable lessons if we reflect on them.

TALK AMONGST YOURSELVES

1. Have you ever been taught about this episode?
2. Which groups in the above history lesson were racist?
3. What does this lesson tell us about racism, individuality, and nobility in America?

TALK #20
IT'S A HASHTAG LIFE

Do you know what an octothorpe is? You do know what the thing is, but you might not know the label. I hereby present the octothorpe: #. You have seen one at the head of every main section in this book. Telephony gave us the term, and most people have called it a pound sign for a long time. In this era of social media, people call it a hashtag.

A hashtag is a tool people use to align themselves with viewpoints or pursuits without writing too much verbiage. In media platforms requiring economy with words, an octothorpe is a helpful version of shorthand (look up "shorthand" if you are younger than I am and be amazed).

Twitter, for example, limits a tweet to 280 characters (formerly it was 140). A character is any keystroke. The paragraph above has 279 characters proving that a single tweet does not let you say much. It does, however, let you say it to a lot of people in a lot of places. Therein the benefits and dangers lie.

Link the social media hashtag with social justice. Hashtags let posters contextualize their concerns without having to produce long captions or explanations. A person can undermine that element, however, when ignoring the larger context of an organization to which an octothorpe points. This is where the true story from my life enters the picture.

An evangelical pastor I know and admire led his church to participate in a protest about a social justice issue. He posted a picture of his congregants at the protest. He linked his church to the organization behind the event by using a hashtag. But that organization's website declares decidedly unbiblical views on various significant matters. The pastor did not qualify his link in any way. #boywasItroubled.

Here is the kicker. His post was the impetus for this book. #atleastthatgotmewriting.

Talk amongst yourselves

1. Was that pastor irresponsible in using that hashtag that way?
2. Have you ever linked to an organization without checking on their positions?
3. To what degree should you publicly associate with an organization that stands against biblical teaching?

TALK #21
RECEIVING THE FACE

Do you receive the face? If that question is Greek to you, then you are on the right track. The Apostle James wrote to the church about "favoritism." The components of the colorful Greek word he chose say "to receive the face." That means making judgments based merely on external factors. Receive his words from James 2:1-13.

> My brothers and sisters, do not show favoritism as you hold on to the faith in our glorious Lord Jesus Christ. For if someone comes into your meeting wearing a gold ring and dressed in fine clothes, and a poor person dressed in filthy clothes also comes in, if you look with favor on the one wearing the fine clothes and say, "Sit here in a good place," and yet you say to the poor person, "Stand over there," or "Sit here on the floor by my footstool," haven't you

made distinctions among yourselves and become judges with evil thoughts? Listen, my dear brothers and sisters: Didn't God choose the poor in this world to be rich in faith and heirs of the kingdom that he has promised to those who love him? Yet you have dishonored the poor. Don't the rich oppress you and drag you into court? Don't they blaspheme the good name that was invoked over you? Indeed, if you fulfill the royal law prescribed in the Scripture, "Love your neighbor as yourself," you are doing well. If, however, you show favoritism, you commit sin and are convicted by the law as transgressors. For whoever keeps the entire law, and yet stumbles at one point, is guilty of breaking it all. For he who said, "Do not commit adultery," also said, "Do not murder." So if you do not commit adultery, but you murder, you are a lawbreaker. Speak and act as those who are to be judged by the law of freedom. For judgment is without mercy to the one who has not shown mercy. Mercy triumphs over judgment.

The law of freedom must shape our view of social justice. Justice rules out oppression in the court. Justice and mercy must count in the church, count for the poor, and count for all.

TALK AMONGST YOURSELVES

1. Do you receive the face?
2. Can we make prejudiced distinctions in the church against the rich? Should we tell a rich person to stand aside or sit on the floor?
3. In a church that did not receive the face, could a rich man serve as an elder? Could a poor man be an elder? Could a slave?

TALK #22
THE COMMUNISM CHALLENGE

TRUE STORY

All my young life, the political Red Menace loomed. I was almost two when the Sputnik satellite beeped in earth orbit. In my third year, Nikita Sergeyevich Khrushchev brandished his shoe at the United Nations. I was five during the Cuban Missile Crisis. My grade school taught me to use my durable desk to shelter from a Soviet atomic blast.

Years later, in Bible college, a professor asked our class if we saw red in Acts. He directed our attention to a text and asked if we saw communism. I was alarmed by the mere possibility. Rather than hiding under my desk, I did the reading and the thinking. Study the matter for yourself by reading Acts 4:32-5:11.

> Now the entire group of those who believed were of one heart and mind, and no one claimed that any of his possessions was his own, but instead

they held everything in common. With great power the apostles were giving testimony to the resurrection of the Lord Jesus, and great grace was on all of them. For there was not a needy person among them because all those who owned lands or houses sold them, brought the proceeds of what was sold, and laid them at the apostles' feet. This was then distributed to each person as any had need. Joseph, a Levite from Cyprus by birth, the one the apostles called Barnabas (which is translated Son of Encouragement), sold a field he owned, brought the money, and laid it at the apostles' feet. But a man named Ananias, with his wife Sapphira, sold a piece of property. However, he kept back part of the proceeds with his wife's knowledge, and brought a portion of it and laid it at the apostles' feet. "Ananias," Peter asked, "why has Satan filled your heart to lie to the Holy Spirit and keep back part of the proceeds of the land? Wasn't it yours while you possessed it? And after it was sold, wasn't it at your disposal? Why is it that you planned this thing in your heart? You have not lied to people but to God." When he heard these words, Ananias dropped dead, and a great fear came on all who heard. The young men got up, wrapped his body, carried him out, and buried him. About three hours later, his wife came in, not knowing what had happened. "Tell me," Peter asked her, "did you sell the land for this price?" "Yes," she said, "for that price." Then Peter said to her, "Why did you agree to test the Spirit of the Lord? Look, the feet of those who have buried your husband are at the door, and they will carry you out." Instantly she dropped dead at his feet. When the young men came in, they found her dead, carried her out, and buried her beside her husband. Then great fear came on the whole church and on all who heard these things.

The lesson was not about being better off red than dead. The professor wanted his students to read the Bible carefully. Think about what you just read and relate it to social justice.

TALK AMONGST YOURSELVES

1. Does this passage undermine ownership of private property?
2. Is this pooled property approach a mandatory model for the church? Do you see it beyond the early chapters of Acts?
3. Does this passage support government redistribution of wealth?
4. How does this example of generosity challenge you?

TALK #23
THE WEDDING PLANNERS

TRUE STORY

Preparing for my sister's wedding included setting a date, reserving the church sanctuary, hiring a photographer, choosing music, and finding a place for the reception. All of that activity is standard operating procedure. We did not expect, however, that approaching the happy date would include passing through a military operation.

My sister married in the summer of 1967. Riots blighted Newark that season. Our apartment sat two-and-a-half miles from the worst of the violence and devastation, but the terrible tension pervaded all neighborhoods.

The spring season proved challenging as tension mounted. The following year, after Martin Luther King Jr was assassinated, one White kid in school said his family was celebrating the murder. Other

White kids, including me, were shocked by the deed and the comment.

Back to our wedding planning in the summer of 1967. The bridal party gowns waited in a shop in a commercial zone full of mom-and-pop type stores and mid-size businesses. The stores served the whole community. We feared that the area would suffer looting and burning, so we rushed to grab the gowns. We saw National Guard troops posted with rifles. Military helicopters hovered overhead. I was an 11-year-old as I absorbed the sad spectacle. I will never forget it.

Oddly, the bridal shop was one of a few stores on the block not pillaged and burned when the riot broke. I guess those clothes were too formal for the occasion or perhaps bore the wrong color. Some businesses never bounced back. Deep scars remain half a century later.

In late July, our family donned our wedding finery. We witnessed two become one and enjoyed a great party at a modest reception hall. We have pictures to commemorate a bright spot in a clouded summer.

God showed the Apostle John events yet in the future, and John recorded them for us. In Revelation 21, we approach a grand wedding reception having passed through the ultimate war zone. Nations are in an uproar. God's judgment falls on all types of unrepentant sinners. Yet, the church, the bride of Christ, verges on the ultimate wedding party. The bride includes people of all ethnicities who hold only one thing in common: salvation from sin and judgment by the work of Jesus, the most august Bridegroom.

The church has to navigate tough terrain in our troubled times. Do it as the ultimate wedding planners. Approach everything happening now through the justice, truth, and grace of our Bridegroom.

TALK AMONGST YOURSELVES

1. How would you process your business being looted or burnt?
2. Were the riots beneficial to the city of Newark and its citizens? What would have been a better approach for all to have taken?
3. How does the multi-ethnic wedding feast ahead shape how you see and treat people of all races?
4. How does gospel hope mitigate your worries?

CONCLUSION
TWO ENDINGS

In preceding pages, I expressed some hard things about my paternal grandfather. But he had good points. For example, I could not afford college, and my parents did not have assets to back a student loan. My grandfather served as the guarantor of my debt so I could enroll. Even though he was not a believer, he wanted me to attend Bible college.

Here comes the first ending. It is my grandfather's legacy. Sin wastes years, and my grandfather wasted many. He died at 93. It would have been great to look back on decades of noble living. We could not. That is a sad ending to a long life.

The second ending is a happy one. It has to do with Jesus. It covers my grandfather's greatest debt and mine.

Our purpose is to worship God in all of life. We all owe God that honor as our creator. Like all sinners, my grandfather and I were in spiritual default on that weighty obligation. Jesus died to save sinners like us. What looked like the end of the Lord's life in Jerusalem was the basis of eternal life for us.

At the age of 93, my grandfather placed his faith in Jesus as savior. He ended his life as a rescued sinner.

I had shared the gospel with him various times over the years. He listened courteously but never budged. He came to trust Jesus for salvation at a church in Irvington New Jersey near his senior residence. I was a tad skeptical when he told me that. Yet, his testimony was clear and compelling. I beheld a work of God.

My grandfather's long-term prejudices encompassed Jewish people. Years before he came to faith, I told him that Jesus was Jewish. He was stunned but trusted my training, which he had financially backed! The Lord being Jewish is not a trade secret, but my grandfather had somehow missed that news. By God's grace, he eventually turned to the Jewish Messiah for rescue from guilt and hell. His attitude shifted gloriously by God's grace for the short time he had left.

My grandfather's funeral was a happy occasion. What would have been a difficult funeral became a celebration of saving grace. It made my rookie debut as a funeral officiant an easy assignment and a joy. I hardly needed to write anything. By quoting all the things he said to me about his repentance and conversion, I made the gospel clear to all at the service.

My grandfather is with the Lord now. Jesus is the sole guarantor of my grandfather's resurrection yet to come. Mine too. My grandfather never had to pay the bank for my student loan debt. I cleared my obligation over time. Neither of us could ever clear our debt as sinners. Jesus gets all the credit.

The good news of eternal salvation is the best true story ever told. On the cross, divine justice and mercy combined spectacularly. Social justice (rightly conceived and practiced) helps people. Saving justice rescues sinners. To God be the glory.

It is not fashionable these days to declare the old-time gospel. But we must not permit anything (including the fight for justice on earth) to obscure the cross of Jesus as the remedy for wrath and the source of new life. To lose sight of that glory does injustice to God.

I close with God's words on the matter. He conveyed them through the Apostle Paul.

Romans 1:16-17: I am not ashamed of the gospel, because it is the power of God for salvation to everyone who believes, first to the Jew, and also to the Greek. For in it the righteousness of God is revealed from faith to faith, just as it is written: "The righteous will live by faith."

Romans 3:22-26: The righteousness of God is through faith in Jesus Christ to all who believe, since there is no distinction. For all have sinned and fall short of the glory of God; they are justified freely by his grace through the redemption that is in Christ Jesus. God presented him as the mercy seat by his blood, through faith, to demonstrate his righteousness, because in his restraint God passed over the sins previously committed. God presented him to demonstrate his righteousness at the present time, so that he would be just and justify the one who has faith in Jesus.

Romans 10:9-13: If you confess with your mouth, "Jesus is Lord," and believe in your heart that God raised him from the dead, you will be saved. One believes with the heart, resulting in righteousness, and one confesses with the mouth, resulting in salvation. For the Scripture says, "Everyone who believes on him will not be put to shame, "since there is no distinction between Jew and Greek, because the same Lord of all richly blesses all who call on him. For "everyone who calls on the name of the Lord will be saved."

APPENDIX ONE
GOD'S DIRECTIONS
FOR CONVERSATION

Take time and ponder God's word about our words.

Ephesians 4:17-32: Therefore, I say this and testify in the Lord: You should no longer walk as the Gentiles do, in the futility of their thoughts. They are darkened in their understanding, excluded from the life of God, because of the ignorance that is in them and because of the hardness of their hearts. They became callous and gave themselves over to promiscuity for the practice of every kind of impurity with a desire for more and more. But that is not how you came to know Christ, assuming you heard about him and were taught by him, as the truth is in Jesus, to take off your former way of life, the old self that is corrupted by deceitful desires, to be renewed in the spirit of your minds, and to put on the new self, the one created according to God's likeness in righteousness and purity of the truth. Therefore, putting away lying, "speak the truth, each one to his neighbor," because we are members of one another. "Be angry and do not sin." Don't let the sun go down on your anger, and don't give the devil an opportunity. Let the thief no longer steal. Instead, he is to do honest work with his own hands, so that he has something to share with anyone in need. No foul language should come from your mouth, but only what is good for building up someone in need, so that it gives grace to those who hear. And don't grieve God's Holy Spirit. You were sealed by him for the day of redemption. Let all bitterness, anger and wrath, shouting and slander be removed from you, along with all malice. And be kind and compassionate to one another, forgiving one another, just as God also forgave you in Christ.

Colossians 3:1-17: So if you have been raised with Christ, seek the things above, where Christ is, seated at the right hand of God. Set your minds on things above, not on earthly things. For you died, and your life is hidden with Christ in God. When Christ, who is your life, appears, then you also will appear with him in glory. Therefore, put to death what belongs to your earthly nature: sexual immorality, impurity, lust, evil desire, and greed, which is idolatry. Because of these, God's wrath is coming upon the disobedient, and you once walked in these things when you were living in them. But now, put away all the following: anger, wrath, malice, slander, and filthy language from your mouth. Do not lie to one another, since you have put off the old self with its practices and have put on the new self. You are being renewed in knowledge according to the image of your Creator. In Christ there is not Greek and Jew, circumcision and uncircumcision, barbarian, Scythian, slave and free; but Christ is all and in all. Therefore, as God's chosen ones, holy and dearly loved, put on compassion, kindness, humility, gentleness, and patience, bearing with one another and forgiving one another if anyone has a grievance against another. Just as the Lord has forgiven you, so you are also to forgive. Above all, put on love, which is the perfect bond of unity. And let the peace of Christ, to which you were also called in one body, rule your hearts. And be thankful. Let the word of Christ dwell richly among you, in all wisdom teaching and admonishing one another through psalms, hymns, and spiritual songs, singing to God with gratitude in your hearts. And whatever you do, in word or in deed, do everything in the name of the Lord Jesus, giving thanks to God the Father through him.

James 1:19-27: My dear brothers and sisters, understand this: Everyone should be quick to listen, slow to speak, and slow to anger, for human anger does not accomplish God's righteousness. Therefore, ridding yourselves of all moral filth and the evil that is so prevalent, humbly receive the implanted word, which is able to save your souls. But be doers of the word and not hearers only, deceiving yourselves. Because if anyone is a hearer of the word and not a doer, he is like someone looking at his own face in a mirror. For he looks at himself, goes away, and immediately forgets what kind of person he was. But the one who looks intently into the perfect law of freedom and perseveres in it, and is not a forgetful hearer but a doer who works—this person will be blessed in what he does. If anyone thinks he is religious without controlling his tongue, his religion is useless and he deceives himself. Pure and undefiled religion before God the Father is this: to look after orphans and widows in their distress and to keep oneself unstained from the world.

1Peter 3:8-12: Finally, all of you be like-minded and sympathetic, love one another, and be compassionate and humble, not paying back evil for evil or insult for insult but, on the contrary, giving a blessing, since you were called for this, so that you may inherit a blessing. For "the one who wants to love life and to see good days, let him keep his tongue from evil and his lips from speaking deceit, and let him turn away from evil and do what is good. Let him seek peace and pursue it, because the eyes of the Lord are on the righteous and his ears are open to their prayer. But the face of the Lord is against those who do what is evil."

Spend time praying about these divine directives before you read this book.

APPENDIX TWO
SOME CORE CONVICTIONS

The following statements are the conceptual neighborhood from which I approach the task at hand. I have no intention of moving from the neighborhood.

The one living God eternally exists as the Father, the Son, and the Holy Spirit. The three persons of the Trinity are equal in perfection. They work harmoniously (though distinctly) in creation, providence, and salvation.

God guided human authors to write the 66 books of the Old Testament and New Testament according to their styles, but the words express his eternal message without deficiency, excess, or error in any part. The Bible is the standard by which all human philosophies, creeds, and conduct must be tested. We must do more than pick favorite passages to advance our plans; we must see the panorama of the Bible to appreciate our place in God's plan.

Sin is rebellion against our creator, who has every right to our love and complete obedience. Sin includes acts of commission and omission, whether in thought, word, attitude, or action. Sin is more than broken rules; it is a broken relationship with God. Every human being is a sinner, and every aspect of our being is affected by sin. Sin results in death and eternal conscious punishment and is a problem beyond human resolution. All human beings are sinners by nature and practice. Though fallen, all human beings have value by bearing the image of God and are worthy of protection and just treatment from the moment of conception to the moment of death.

Jesus died on the cross as our sinless substitute, taking the wrath we deserved, and offering the worship and obedience we have all failed to give God. The same body that died on the cross emerged from the tomb in perfect form, never to die again. Jesus ascended to the place of highest authority and is ruler over all creation. Until he returns, there will be no perfect world.

Salvation is a gift that includes a new righteous standing before God as the top judge, a new heart orientation toward God as holy Father, a new relationship with God that matures by the work of the Holy Spirit, and a perfect future in which we will fully share the resurrection power of Jesus the Son. Salvation from sin is based on grace alone, received by faith alone, and is found in Jesus alone. Salvation is not an ineffective gift. We will never be perfect in this life, but we must grow in our appreciation of the gift giver and reflect that growth in changed lives.

The church is composed of all who have faith in the saving work of Jesus Christ and who have been given eternal life by the Holy Spirit. The church passes the boundaries of history and geography to unite all saved sinners into one body, of which Christ is the head. A working distinction between the invisible church (composed of all true believers) and the visible church (the earthly gathering which may include unbelievers) is presently useful, but in the end, this distinction will vanish. Christ builds his one church by establishing local churches. Saved sinners are no better than anyone, but we are better off by God's grace. Pride has no place in a healthy local church. Jesus alone is our boast.

Truth is not merely a social construct, and language is not simply a tool for political power. We must embrace everything God's word teaches. That is the way for the church to serve as salt and light in any society. We should interpret the Bible according to the plain sense of the text, paying attention to the context and type of literature.

Every local church in every age and place exists in a culture that both helps and hinders ministry. Responsible ministry appreciates both the benefits a culture provides and the dangers it poses. We can use helpful tools a culture provides, but we must lovingly confront all cultures with the Lordship of Christ.

Our reason for being is to worship God. Worship is a humble orientation of the whole person to God, expressed in all of life. We worship God by serving him and by serving others in his name. Salvation enables people to live on purpose.

A WORD OF THANKS

I thank my parents for setting a good example despite the hardships they endured and the obstacles they overcame. They are now richer than they ever could have imagined, with more to come in the resurrection! Many thanks to my sister for protecting her little brother many times. Once she risked a razor slash to the face to keep me safe.

My wife Francine and daughter Jacey happily grant me time alone to write that could have been theirs. Jacey ably tackles tedious tasks as my assistant. My son Jonathan hones my thinking about many things, especially economics and ethics. My grandchildren Hudson, Felicity, and Claire prove that there are more important and entertaining things than books.

Jess Rainer supplied valuable direction, resources, and encouragement. I appreciate the support of the C242 family. David and Natalie Bush have been almost as enthusiastic about my work as my parents would be! David, Natalie, Sean Twohig, Becky Ward, and Christine Yalanis were valuable advance readers. Beth Morgan once again brought her editing talent to the table. Remaining mistakes or blemishes belong to me, not to them.

Most of all I thank God the Son for solving my biggest justice problem, God the Father for sending him, and God the Holy Spirit for opening my eyes. Soli Deo Gloria.

ALSO BY THE AUTHOR

The Corporate Prayer Challenge:
30 Days to Kickstart the Change We Need

Available through Amazon

Made in the USA
Middletown, DE
28 November 2020

25526880R00076